*I want to thank you, Son,
for all you've given me...
and let you know that
one of the greatest gifts of all
is the joy that has been mine
ever since the moment
I first held you in my arms.*

— Deanne Laura Gilbert

Other books in this series...

Blue Mountain Arts.

A Friend Lives in Your Heart Forever

A Mother Is Love

I Love You Soooo Much
by Douglas Pagels

I'd Love to Give These Gifts to You

Keep Believing in Yourself and Your Special Dreams

Promises To Myself

Sister, You Have a Special Place in My Heart

The Greatest Gift of All Is... A Daughter like You

The Greatest Gift of All Is...

A Son
like You

Words to Share with a Wonderful Son

SPS Studios™
Boulder, Colorado

Library of Congress Catalog Card Number: 2001005522
ISBN: 0-88396-612-3

We wish to thank Susan Polis Schutz for permission to reprint the following poems that appear in this publication: "To My Son, I Love You," "My Son, I Hope that All Your Dreams Become a Reality, and I Love You," and "My Son, Always Remember How Proud I Am of You and How Much I Love You." Copyright © 1988, 1989, 1991 by Stephen Schutz and Susan Polis Schutz. All rights reserved.

ACKNOWLEDGMENTS appear on page 48.

Certain trademarks are used under license.

Manufactured in Thailand
Third Printing: 2003

This book is printed on recycled paper.

Library of Congress Cataloging-in-Publication Data

The greatest gift of all is — a son like you : words to share with a wonderful son.
        p. cm.
   ISBN 0-88396-612-3 (hardcover : alk. paper)
   1. Sons—Quotations, maxims, etc. 2. Conduct of life—Quotations, maxims, etc. I. SPS Studios.
   PN6084.S67 G74 2001
   306.874—dc21

                                                        2001005522
                                                              CIP

SPS Studios, Inc.
P.O. Box 4549, Boulder, Colorado 80306

Contents

(Authors listed in order of first appearance)

Son, Remember This...

I'll always love you. Remember... as you read these words, that I'll hold you in a very precious place in my heart — not just today, but as long as there are stars in the sky.

Remember that — if I could — I would give you the moon and the sun in return for all the smiles and memories you've given me.

And remember that when I say "I love you," I want you to know what those words really mean. "I love you" means that you're the most wonderful son there could ever be. It means that you have made me more proud of you than you could even begin to imagine. And it means that I will never let a day go by without feeling blessed by the giving... of a gift like you.

— Laurel Atherton

What Is a Son?

A son is a warm spot in your heart and a smile on your lips.

In the beginning, he is charmingly innocent, putting his complete trust in you. He comes to you for a hand to hold and for the security only your arms can provide. He shares his tales of adventure and knows how proud you are of his discoveries and accomplishments. All his problems can be solved by a hug and a kiss from you, and the bond you share is so strong it is almost tangible.

Time passes, and your innocent little boy starts to test his limits. He lets go of your hand to race into the midst of life without thinking ahead or looking both ways. His problems have grown along with him, and he has learned that you can't always make his life better or kiss his troubles away. He spends much of his time away from you, and though you long for the closeness you once shared, he chooses independence and privacy.

Discoveries and accomplishments aren't as easy to come by now, and sometimes he wonders about his worth. But you know the worth of that young man. He is your past and your future. He is hopes and dreams that have made it through each and every disappointment and failure.

In your heart, your son is precious and treasured. Together, you struggled through the years to find the right amount of independence for each new stage of his life, until finally, you had to learn to let him go. Now you put your trust in him, leaving that son whom you hold so dear totally in his own care. You hope he always remembers that you have a hand for him to hold and arms to provide comfort or support.

Most of all, you hope that he believes in himself as much as you believe in him, and that he knows how much you love him.

— Barbara Cage

Son, right before my eyes, you have grown up so much on your way to becoming the special person you are today.

From a baby, to a boy, to a young man, you were full of life and filled with surprises. Trying to keep up with you has been many things: rewarding, challenging, hopeful, and fulfilling. In every one of your years, you have given me more happiness and love than most people will ever dream of.

As a family, we have walked along many paths on our way from yesterday to where we are today. Love has always been our companion, keeping us close even when we've been apart.

You have given me many gifts on that journey. But none are more precious, Son, than the smiles you give to my heart.

— Marin McKay

I Remember, Son...

Your years of growing,
all our shared thoughts and feelings,
the carefree and happy times a family shares.
I remember the joy, the tears, and the sorrow —
stormy emotions for changing times.
I remember the squeeze of your hand,
whispered "I love you's,"
the snapshots and memories
of time and years.
I remember all the ways
you've kept my life busy.
Every day, I celebrate and honor
all the ways you make my heart proud.

You, Son, are loving memories,
close and strong and celebrated.

— Linda E. Knight

My Son, Always Remember How Proud I Am of You and How Much I Love You

You are growing up to be
an incredible young man
You are very unique and special
and I know that
your talents will give you
many paths to choose from
in the future
As you grow up, my son
always keep your many interests —
they will keep you
constantly occupied
Always keep your positive outlook —
it will give you the energy to
accomplish great things
Always keep your determination —
it will give you the ability
to succeed in meeting your goals

Always keep your excitement
about whatever you do —
it will help you to have fun
Always keep your sense of humor —
it will allow you to
make mistakes and learn from them
Always keep your confidence —
it will allow you to take risks
and not be afraid of failure
Always keep your sensitivity —
it will help you to understand
and do something about
injustices in the world
As you continue to grow
in your own unique, wonderful way
always remember that
I am more proud of you
than ever before and
I love you

— Susan Polis Schutz

In life, my son, there will always be
    many paths to follow;
I hope you always choose the right one.
If you give a part of yourself to life,
the part you receive back
    will be so much greater.
Never regret the past, but learn by it.
Never lose sight of your dreams;
a person who can dream
    will always have hope.
Believe in yourself;
    if you do, everyone else will.
You have the ability to accomplish anything,
but never do it at someone else's expense.
If you can go through life loving others,
you will have achieved
    the greatest success of all.

— Judy LeSage

Son, If I Could Have Anything in the World...

I'd wish that you would always be happy,
forever healthy, and that your life would be filled
   with all the things that bring you laughter and love.
I wish for you a life where your dreams come true
   and your goals are achieved;
I wish that I could always
   wipe any tears from your face
and make everything okay again.
I hope you will always know
   that I am thinking about you
and forever wanting nothing more
   than your complete happiness in life.
It's your happiness that brings me such immense joy,
because you are my son
   and I love you so much.

— Shelly Gross

Someone Cares About You, and That Someone Is Me!

If you're wondering whether anyone is thinking about you now, caring about what you're doing, wishing you the best, and remembering you in prayer...

If you're feeling alienated from the world, with no one on your side, and you're questioning if there's another human being who would even be concerned about what's going on in your life...

Well, wonder no more. Someone is thinking of you and someone does care about you, and that someone is me.

If you're wishing you had someone who hopes that life is being good to you, that you're coping well with every challenge and reaching the goals you want to reach...

If you're hoping that there is someone in your corner of
the world that you could call on any time, someone
with whom you could share your hopes and dreams
and disappointments...

Well, don't waste your time wishing and wondering
anymore. I'd be glad to be that someone. All you
have to do is let me know and I'll be there.

If you need someone to talk to, to share your worries
with, to wish for you perfect health, prosperity, and
peace and happiness...

If you want someone to point out your good qualities
because you just need lifting up, someone who would
be on your side no matter what and who would go
with you whatever distance you have to go...

Then look no further than my direction, and don't give
it a second thought. Know that someone is thinking
of you and someone cares about you, and that
someone is me.

— Donna Fargo

I remember when you were so tiny
that I could cradle you in my arms
and watch you sleep —
so oblivious to the world.
When you awoke, you'd smile at me
and curl all your fingers
around one of mine,
and hold on so very tightly
that I thought you'd never let go.
Those same precious fingers
wound themselves around
   my heart, too...
and to this day,
they have never let go.

— Maria Shockley Erman

Twelve Tips to Help You Through Life

1. *Shine*... with your God-given talents.
2. *Sparkle*... with interest when you listen to others.
3. *Twinkle*... with a sense of humor, and never take life too seriously.
4. *Sing*... to keep up your spirits.
5. *Pray*... and you'll know you're never alone.
6. *Unwrap*... your dreams and make them happen.
7. *Celebrate*... your every step to success.
8. *Decorate*... your own space and make it your peaceful retreat.
9. *Play*... with passion after you work hard.
10. *Exchange*... your doubts for hopes, your frowns for smiles.
11. *Make*... cookies, friends, happiness.
12. *Believe*... in the spirit of life and in your power to make the world a better place.

— Jacqueline Schiff

Son, I've Always Had So Many Wishes for You

When you were so small, I wished
   you could talk.
As you struggled to crawl, I wished
   you could walk.
When your room was so messy,
   I wished it were neat.
While you played with your food,
   I wished you would eat.
When you learned how to drive,
   I wished you would wait.
I wished you home safely,
   not out on a date.

And now, as I've watched you
   become a young man,
setting out on your own to learn
   all that you can
from books and from life,
   I want you to know
I stand proudly behind you,
   wherever you go.
I have dreams for you and one wish,
   just one:
I wish we had more time together,
   my son.

— Diane Sieverson

The Bond Between Parent and Son Lasts a Lifetime

It remains unchanged by time or distance. It is the purest love — unconditional and true. It is understanding of any situation and forgiving of any mistake.

It creates a support that is constant while everything else changes. It is a friendship based on mutual love, respect, and a genuine liking of each other as a person.

It is knowing that no matter where you go or who you are, there is someone who truly loves you and is always there to support and console you. When a situation seems impossible, you make it through together by holding on to each other.

The bond between parent and son is strong enough to withstand harsh words and hurt feelings, for it is smart enough to always see the love beyond the words.

It is brave enough to always speak the truth, even when lies would be easier. It is always there — anytime, anywhere — whenever it is needed. It is a gift held in the heart and in the soul, and it cannot be taken away or exchanged for another.

To possess this love is a treasure that makes life more valuable.

— Stephanie Douglass

Son, I Want to Share These Thoughts with You

No matter where you go in this world,
here are a few things
I hope you'll remember...

Always hold honor as a high virtue. Despite
how the world may be, rise above.
Always speak the truth, because others
will hold you in high esteem as a man
who can be trusted.
Never lose faith in your fellow human
beings, despite times when they may let
you down. Never forget to thank God
for the opportunities you've been given.

Believe in hard work. No one will hand you
the future you want. The ladder to success is
steep, but take one step at a time and you'll
get to the top.
No matter where you go or what mistakes
you make, remember that your family will
always be here for you. That's how deep
love goes.
Always believe in yourself. Your happiness
depends on no one else but you. If there is
something that you are unhappy about, you
must change it.
Always hold love close to you. When you
make a commitment, cherish it for the rest
of your life.

— Sherrie L. Householder

Know What It Means
to Be a Man, My Son...

A man is someone who realizes
   that strength of character
is more important than being tough.
He can be tender and kind,
   and he doesn't misuse his authority.
He is generous and enjoys giving
   as well as receiving.
He is understanding;
   he tries to see both sides
      of a situation.

A man is responsible;
he knows what needs to be done,
and he does it.
He is trustworthy;
his word is his honor.
He loves humor and he looks
at the bright side of things.
He takes time to think
before he reacts.
He loves life, nature, discovery,
excitement, and so much more.
He is a little boy sometimes,
living in an adult body
and enjoying the best of both worlds.

— Barbara Cage

True Greatness

A man is as great as the dreams he dreams,
   As great as the love he bears,
As great as the values he redeems,
   And the happiness he shares.
A man is as great as the thoughts he thinks,
   As the worth he has attained,
As the fountains at which his spirit drinks,
   And the insight he has gained.
A man is as great as the truth he speaks,
   As great as the help he gives,
As great as the destiny he seeks,
   As great as the life he lives.

— C. E. Flynn

Always Be True to Yourself

Throughout your life, I hope you will always
pursue sensitivity and kindness
   as your chosen way.
Your sense of humor is wonderful;
   hold on to it.
Being able to laugh at the world
   will see you through many hard times.
Guard against bitterness and sarcasm;
   they can destroy you.
Be yourself; the world will benefit
   from your talent and your humor.
Search for people who love and
   appreciate you for who you are
and who encourage you to improve.
Don't be satisfied with less
   than all you can be,
for you have greatness within you.

— Bill Cross

My Son, I Hope that All Your Dreams Become a Reality, and I Love You

Dreams can come true if you take the time to
think about what you want in life…
Get to know yourself
Find out who you are
Choose your goals carefully
Be honest with yourself
But don't think about yourself so much
that you analyze every word and action
Don't become preoccupied with yourself
Find many interests and pursue them
Find out what is important to you
Find out what you are good at
Don't be afraid to make mistakes
Work hard to achieve successes
When things are not going right
don't give up — just try harder
Find courage inside of you to remain strong
Give yourself freedom to try out new things

Don't be so set in your ways that you can't grow
Always act in an ethical way
Laugh and have a good time
Form relationships with people you respect
Treat others as you want them to treat you
Be honest with people
Accept the truth
Speak the truth
Open yourself up to love
Don't be afraid to love
Remain close to your family
Take part in the beauty of nature
Be appreciative of all that you have
Help those less fortunate than you
Try to make other lives happy
Work towards peace in the world
Live life to the fullest
My son, dreams can come true
and I hope that all your dreams become a reality
I love you

— Susan Polis Schutz

To My Son

I have loved
watching you go through life
as only a child can...
    laughing, crying,
        so sure of yourself,
and at the same time
        so often full of doubts.
My heart broke for you
        when life was unfair;
I would have shielded you
from pain and heartache
        if you had let me.

I wanted to protect you,
but you needed to grow
into your own person,
so I had to let go of you —
a little at a time.
That was one of the hardest
things I've ever had to do.

Your childhood is gone now,
    and I still miss those wonderful times,
but I am so proud of
the adult you have become.
I love you,
and whatever paths in life
you may choose to embrace,
    my love will be with you...
and I will cherish you always.

— Peggy Selig

In Admiration of You, My Son

If someone were to ask me what has been
   my biggest accomplishment in life,
I would lift my head high and speak
   from my heart with a parent's pride
as I said the words "my son."
I would speak about the good fortune
   and blessing of having a son
who spreads happiness and comfort
to all who cross his path;
a son who puts the concerns of others
   ahead of his own;
a son who has grown from
   an enchanting young boy
into a compassionate, courageous man;
a son who has grown up knowing
the value of respect
and who has earned the admiration
   of those who know him.

You have so many wonderful qualities
that my words to describe them
     would be endless —
much like my pride in you.
You have given so much joy
     to my life,
and I am overcome with feelings
     of tranquillity
whenever I think about who and what
     you've become.
You are my biggest and greatest
     accomplishment.
You have given my life more meaning
     and happiness
than you could ever know.
I love you.

— Andrea Adaire Fischer

Though You Have Grown,
I Will Carry You
in My Heart Always

A long time ago
you held out your hand to me.
Gripping it softly,
I grabbed hold of your heart,
and I knew it became a part of me forever.
In a moment's time,
I felt I held the world in my hands.
But as I watched the way
your eyes wandered curiously
and the way your tiny body
twisted and curled,
I knew the day would come
when you wouldn't fit in my arms any longer
and I would be left with no choice
but to loosen my grasp and let you go.

Though it is hard to watch
you grow up so quickly,
every day I feel the pride that comes
with being your parent
and knowing that I have played a part
in bringing you into this world.
You amaze me each day
as you set goals
and accomplish feats,
brightening the lives of others
with your caring heart
and beautiful smile.
And though I can no longer
hold you in my arms,
I will carry you in my heart
each day of my life.

— Deana Marino

My Son, Never Forget How Much I Love You

When you were very, very small,
I used to dance with you cradled in my arms.
You were my precious angel,
and when I held you close,
love overwhelmed me.

I used to wonder what kind of life you would lead.
What would be your first word, your first job?
What kind of man would you become?
And would your life take you far away from me?

Then I'd hold you even closer.
I'd give you an extra kiss and an extra squeeze,
and whisper "I love you" one more time.
I knew you were too young to remember my words,
but I prayed you would never forget them.

Now you are a man.
There are days when I still long
    to cradle you in my arms
and dance with you once again.
Although I miss my little boy,
I am so proud of the man you are
and of who you will become.
When I think of you,
love still overwhelms me.
And as we both grow older
and memories fade,
please never forget these words
that you were once too small
    to remember:
"I love you."

— Kathryn Higginbottom Gorin

Poems to Help My Son Be Strong
Along the Path of Life

"Always keep your goodness
and never lose your love.
For then, Son, you'll be
rewarded with success
in ways you never dreamed of."

"You can be head and shoulders above the crowd.
You don't have to be a giant to be strong.
Walk tall and be proud. All you have to be...
is someone people look up to."

"In the course of time, you will be reminded that hard
work gets good results and keeping healthy is essential.
Know when to work your mind and let your body relax,
and know when doing just the opposite makes the most
sense. Being able to handle whatever life brings your way
is not a matter of coincidence."

"You've already got a good idea of what is expected of you and wished for you. One of the best things you can accomplish on life's pathway is to be a walking example of the golden rule. Don't let anyone fool you into thinking that it is worthless; it is one of the most valuable things you can do."

"You've got so many possibilities ahead! Don't be too quick to limit your choices of what to do, because you might limit your chances of unimagined joys that are waiting just for you."

"You've got a wonderful sense of humor and a good outlook on life. Let those qualities help to see you through when you're deciding where to go and you're not sure what to do."

"You've got a big heart. Keep it filled with happiness. You've got a fascinating mind. Keep finding new ways to grow. Keep yearning. Keep learning. Keep trying. Keep smiling. And keep remembering that a parent's love goes with you... everywhere you go."

— Douglas Richards

To My Son, I Love You

I feel so fortunate to have you for a son
I love your bright face
when we talk seriously about the world
I love your smile
when you laugh at the inconsistencies in the world
I love your eyes
when you are showing emotion
I love your mind
when you are discovering new ideas
and creating dreams to follow

Many people tell me that
they cannot talk to their children
that they cannot wait for them to leave home
I want you to know
that I enjoy you so much and
I look forward to any time we can spend together
Not only are you my adored son
but you are also my friend
I am so proud of you
my son and
I love you

— Susan Polis Schutz

I'm Your Biggest Fan!

I am so proud of you
and I love you so much!
You're more than just a
fantastic part of our family...
you are a special,
one-in-a-million kind of person...
who is on the way to getting a little closer,
each and every day,
to the dreams you want to realize.

And, Son, I hope you'll
always remember...

I don't just THINK that
the earth and the stars revolve
around you.

I am absolutely
SURE that they do!

— Ceal Carson

You're Everything
a Son Should Be

Throughout your life, I have seen how each and
every step that you took led you away from me
and toward your independence. Yet often, you
didn't even notice that it was occurring.

The memories I have of you still stir in my heart.
Sometimes, they cause me to stop what I'm doing
and regret the quick passage of time. I'm amazed
that my little boy now looks out at me from a
grown man's body.

As you move on to new adventures, I'll be there
to support you and believe in you. I am so proud
of all that you've accomplished; you've become
the type of man I always hoped you would be.
(I just wish it hadn't happened so fast!)

— Barbara Cage

The Greatest
Gift of All Is...

A Son like You

In your lifetime, you have given me
far more gifts than I can count;
yet the ones I remember most
are the ones you gave from within,
often without even realizing it.

When you were a child,
you gave me the gift
of allowing me to see the world
through your eyes,
and finding beauty
   I had overlooked before.

The many memories we've made,
the love you have given,
    and the love I have for you
are lifetime gifts.

I want to thank you for all
    you've given me,
and let you know that
    one of the greatest gifts of all
is the joy that has been mine
    ever since the moment
        I first held you in my arms.

— Deanne Laura Gilbert

ACKNOWLEDGMENTS

The following is a partial list of authors whom the publisher especially wishes to thank for permission to reprint their works.

PrimaDonna Entertainment Corp. for "Someone Cares About You, and That Someone Is Me!" by Donna Fargo. Copyright © 2001 by PrimaDonna Entertainment Corp. All rights reserved.

Diane Sieverson for "Son, I've Always Had So Many Wishes for You." Copyright © 2002 by Diane Sieverson. All rights reserved.

A careful effort has been made to trace the ownership of poems used in this anthology in order to obtain permission to reprint copyrighted materials and give proper credit to the copyright owners. If any error or omission has occurred, it is completely inadvertent, and we would like to make corrections in future editions provided that written notification is made to the publisher:

SPS STUDIOS, INC., P.O. Box 4549, Boulder, Colorado 80306.